Dear Granny,

LETTERS BETWEEN GENERATIONS

By Anne H. Adams

ISBN 0-7414-5807-1

Published by:
INFINITY
PUBLISHING.COM
1094 New DeHaven Street, Suite 100
West Conshohocken, PA 19428-2713
Info@buybooksontheweb.com
www.buybooksontheweb.com
Toll-free (877) BUY-BOOK
Local Phone (610) 941-9999
Fax (610) 941-9959

Printed in the United States of America

Published March 2010

"Sisters, sisters, there were never such devoted sisters..."

For Sheila Herzig Shiffman and Finnie Herzig Mandelcorn and their namesakes.

Introduction

This collection of "Dear Granny" and "Dear Jordy" letters is a work of fiction. I have four beloved grandchildren, but I am not this Granny and they are not Jordy.

Granny and Jordy live miles apart and don't see each other often, yet they nourish a warm bond through their letters. As they correspond over the span of almost a year, their written journey winds through serious concerns, light moments, the intimacy of shared secrets, and broken but repaired trust. Granny and Jordy also exchange a series of jokes, which cement their relationship through humor and levity. In Jordy's letters, you will indirectly meet Jordy's parents, sister Diane, brother Michael, and Jordy's friends Jake, Sarah and Darlene.

In these letters I present a variety of situations that may arise. Not all of these are serious issues or problems – several are light and humorous moments – but as Granny and Jordy correspond, their relationship deepens. Then, when Jordy does have worries or problems, the door is open for Granny to provide guidance that Jordy has grown to trust and value.

Although I have created fictitious letters, these are topics of concern to children – jealousy, bullying, friendships, trying to be popular, trust, privacy, divorce, fear of death – as well as ways to resolve conflicts. Today's children are burdened by many personal and societal challenges, but one thing is crystal clear from the research and from our own personal experiences: Children need someone who listens to them, truly hears them, and responds with wisdom, love, and reassurance, not lectures.

Ideally every child should have a parent to fill this role, but parents are often too limited by time, job concerns, or emotional situations to listen attentively and communicate effectively with their children. In the past, when most families lived near relatives in the same village or city, an aunt, uncle, or grandparent helped to fill the role of the loving, interested adult in a child's life. In today's society, however, we are scattered across states, countries, and even oceans. A child can't run to Granny's house after school for cocoa, cookies, and a chat.

Yet children and grandparents can communicate by phone, email, and the "old-fashioned way" through written letters. Telephone, texting, instant messages, and email are certainly quick and easy and should not be discouraged. But I have chosen to create the correspondence between Granny and Jordy as written letters. It is simply my preference to take pen to paper and to read a letter that I can hold in my hands and keep. I also hope that children would be encouraged to write letters — not necessarily to develop good penmanship, though that is an asset, but also to think as they write. The pace of writing a letter in long-hand seems to give children an opportunity to slow down a bit and think about the ideas and emotions they are putting into words. In our fast-paced society, that's a good and rare thing.

However, I certainly don't want to discourage any other form of communication between grandparents and grandchildren. There are all kinds of ways to correspond. If you can't write a letter, I encourage other grandparents to pick up the phone, boot up your computer and send an email or send a text message on your cell phone. The point is to keep open lines of communication between the generations. Sometimes a grandchild may be busy, preoccupied, or reluctant to have a serious conversation or to write more than a line or two in a note. But don't become discouraged. Keep writing, keep phoning, keep the door open and inject a little humor, as Jordy and Granny do with their jokes.

Everyone has a unique focus. For some, it may be music, sports, photography or a specific hobby. I hope you will find something in common to start the conversation about any topic that interests your grandchild. If you are gently persistent, the relationship can flourish and trust will increase between you, regardless of the distance between the generations.

I sincerely hope that you will enjoy getting to know Granny and Jordy and be inspired by these letters to communicate in whatever format best suits you and your family.

August 3

Dear Granny,

Thank you very much for the briefcase you sent me for my birthday. It is very nice and very practical because school is starting soon and a briefcase is a good gift.

You really are a terrific grandmother for always remembering my birthday.

Love,
Jordy

August 9

Dear Granny,

Michael is a big blabbermouth. I feel really bad that he told you I didn't like the briefcase. That's just not true! It's not that I didn't like it but all my friends wear back packs to school so I must have said something to Mom about it, Michael was listening and right away he blabbed to you. Big brothers are a real pain in the neck.

You give great gifts, Granny. Diane went gaga about the yellow cashmere sweater you sent her. She said it was absolutely gorgeous — and you know how picky Diane is.

Anyways, I'm sorry Michael told you I didn't like your present. I always like and appreciate your presents even if they are not always exactly what I wanted.

Are you mad at me because I told Mom I wanted a back pack instead?

Love,
Jordy

August 13

Dear Jordy,

Of course I'm not mad at you. When I send you a gift I want it to be exactly what you want and that's why I always leave the tag on (without the price) so that you can exchange it for something else. I thought you knew that. I care very much about giving you a birthday gift that you absolutely love. If you want to make it easier for me, please tell me what you would like beforehand and if I can, I'll buy it for you. This way both of us will get exactly what we want.

Love you,
Granny

P.S. Are you looking forward to school?
I hope you get good teachers that you like.

August 20

Dear Granny,

Thank you for your letter. I was afraid you would be mad at me when you found out I wasn't crazy about the briefcase.

Your birthday is coming soon and we are all trying to figure out what to get you. Mom and Dad are sending you opera tickets (don't tell them I told) but Michael said that's boring and I think he's planning to send you a really cool CD. Diane still hasn't gotten a gift but knowing Diane, it will probably be something perfect. I don't have a clue what to get you. Could you give me a hint? It would really help me out. I want to get you something that you really, really, really like.

Love you, Jordy

August 25

Dear Jordy,

How very thoughtful of you to want to get me a gift that I would really, really like. I thought about it and this is what I would appreciate. A DVD. Remember the time when you were five or six and we watched that really funny movie on TV and how we both laughed and laughed. I thought that if you selected a DVD that <u>*you*</u> *like we could watch it together and we would both have a good time. Another gift I'd enjoy is a book – preferably one of your favorite books. It would be interesting to see what kids are reading today and it would be nice to talk about it afterwards.*

Either gift would be the "perfect" gift and I can't wait to see which DVD or book you choose.

Love you, Granny

September 3

Dear Granny,

Did you hear the news? Mom was laid off. I know that sounds like bad news but Mom said she couldn't be happier because she missed not being home and now she can't wait to do all the things she never had time to do.

Mom can't wait to start cooking and baking. She told us that tomorrow we could each have our favorite breakfast. I chose pancakes, Diane chose crepes. Michael said he likes French toast but he doesn't really care and can share the pancakes with me. Dad is sticking with the same breakfast he always has — cereal, toast and coffee. I asked Mom what she is having but she said she doesn't know yet.

I can't wait for breakfast tomorrow...

Love you,
Jordy

P.S. The kitchen smells sooo yummy. Mom is baking chocolate cake. My mouth just drools when I think of all the things she's going to bake.

P.P.S. Good news!!! Jake and Sarah will be in the same class as me.

MOM's
KITCHEN

September 7

Dear Granny,

I'm so glad you're not dead!!!!

When Daddy told me you had a bad car accident my stomach got sick and I just knew you had died. But before I could barf, Daddy told me you were in the hospital and you would get well. I am sooo glad. Mom got a plane ticket right away to go and see you when she heard you had the accident. She just phoned and said you look TERRIBLE. She said it was the first time she realized you were old. And your face looks awful, all black and blue and swollen.

I feel so bad for you. Are you in lots of pain? If there is anything — ANYTHING — I can do please tell me. I'm sure Mom would let me take a plane to cheer you up. I won't cry when I look at you. No matter how old and ugly you look, I will always, ALWAYS, love you.

X♡X♡X♡X
Love,
Jordy

P.S. I hope you like this picture I drew for you. I thought it might cheer you up if you could look at my drawing of your apartment building and the park next door.

Jordy

September 13

Dearest Jordy,

I can't tell you how your letter made me feel!

I took a look at my face in the mirror and had to laugh because I couldn't recognize myself. I laughed because it hurts to cry and because I know I will soon get back to looking like myself again. I appreciate your always loving me no matter how old and ugly I look. But just to clarify, I am really not that old and the reason I look so horrible right now is that my face is bruised and swollen. The doctors have taken lots of tests and they tell me the swelling will soon go down, the bruises will fade, and I will return to my not-so-bad-looking self. Unfortunately my hearing was affected, and that will take a long time to recover. And both my legs were injured, but with the help of a physical therapist, I should be able to walk again soon. So please don't worry – I'll be alright – it will just take a little time.
And being old, or older (I prefer older) is really not that bad.
I can do what I want – most of the time.
I can stay up late at night and watch movies.
I can stay in bed in the morning and read the newspaper.
I can have ice cream whenever I want.

> *"...I have the most precious thing in the world - a loving grandchild who will love me when my "laugh lines" turn into wrinkles..."*

And best of all, I have the most precious thing in the world – a loving grandchild who will love me when my "laugh lines" turn into wrinkles and will offer a shoulder to lean on when old age makes it difficult to walk.

I love you so much. I love, love, love receiving mail from you. Your letters cheer me up and make me smile. Thank you.

Love,
Granny

P.S. I love your drawing. It is in a frame on my night table. Every time I look at it I think of you and smile.

September 20

Dear Jordy,

Finally, finally, I'm home. I can't tell you how grateful I am to your mother for coming for a week to take care of me. And it was nice of you to keep phoning even though I can't hear well since the accident. Actually, I prefer letters to telephone calls – especially YOUR letters. And, as you know, I'm not comfortable with emailing. It feels so mechanical and impersonal.

Life at home has become sort of routine. This is my typical day:

7:00: My temporary housekeeper wakes me up and asks how I feel.

7:03: I tell her – in no uncertain terms, exactly how I feel.

7:05: She immediately leaves the room.

7:30 - 8:00: She brings me steaming hot coffee and buttered toast with both jam and marmalade; plus some medicines.

8:00 - 12:30: Time passes. I watch TV, read magazines, and do crossword puzzles.

12:30: Lunch. I can eat whatever I want and I don't have to count the calories. Unfortunately I lost my taste for chocolate but the good thing is that I'm finally losing weight.

1:00 - 3:00: Nap

3:00 - 4:00: Physical therapist arrives. She gives me a great big cheerful smile and asks how I feel. I tell her! She says "Now, now, we must look at the bright side, mustn't we?" Then she starts pushing my legs this way and that way, ignores my moans and cheerfully reiterates, "No pain, no gain." I detest that woman. Her name is Sadie Irving, but I call her the "S.I." – The Spanish Inquisitor.

4:00 - 6:00: Rest, read newspapers, magazines.

6:00: My temporary helper brings me supper – exactly what I asked for – pancakes. I'd enjoy them more if I could share them with you.

6:30 - 10:00: Doing crossword puzzles, making list of things that need to be done.

Basically, it's not bad. Apart from physical therapy, it doesn't hurt much. The brightest part of the day is when the mail arrives and there is letter or drawing from you. And then I forget all about the dreary day, and my heart sings.

Love,
Granny

September 23

Dear Granny,

I am happy you like my letters. I like your letters too. They are funny in a way. But I don't know if I can write you a lot because I don't always know what to write about. School is boring. There is nothing interesting to write about.

So if I don't write, it's not because I don't love you. It's just because I have nothing to write about.

Love, Jordy

P.S. What's a Spanish Inquisitor?

September 28

Dear Jordy,

When you have trouble thinking of something to write in a letter, why don't you write questions, starting with "Why?"

When I was your age I had a lot of questions beginning with why – silly questions like: Why does a camel have two humps instead of one...? Why are people made in different colors...? And more serious questions like, why do kids get sick and die...? But whether my questions were silly or serious, nobody had the time or patience to answer them.

The advantage of having a grandmother is that she has all the time in the world to listen to questions and answer them as best she can.

And I'll tell you a secret that I never told anyone before: When you were born, I had a dream, a wish, something that I wanted badly. I wanted to be a grandmother who would always be there to listen, to listen to things that bother you, to try to make you feel better when things don't work out the way they should.

So if you think that I could be someone you can count on to listen and answer questions, I would be very honored, and proud – and HAPPY – because that's what grandmothers like to do.

Love,
Granny

P.S. The name "Spanish Inquisitor" is synonymous with torture. That's because they tortured people horribly to make them confess or to make them convert to the Catholic religion. So when I call my physical therapist S.I. for "Spanish Inquisitor," I'm basically saying she likes to torture. That is a total exaggeration, of course, but that's the way I feel sometimes when she pushes me to the limit of my endurance.

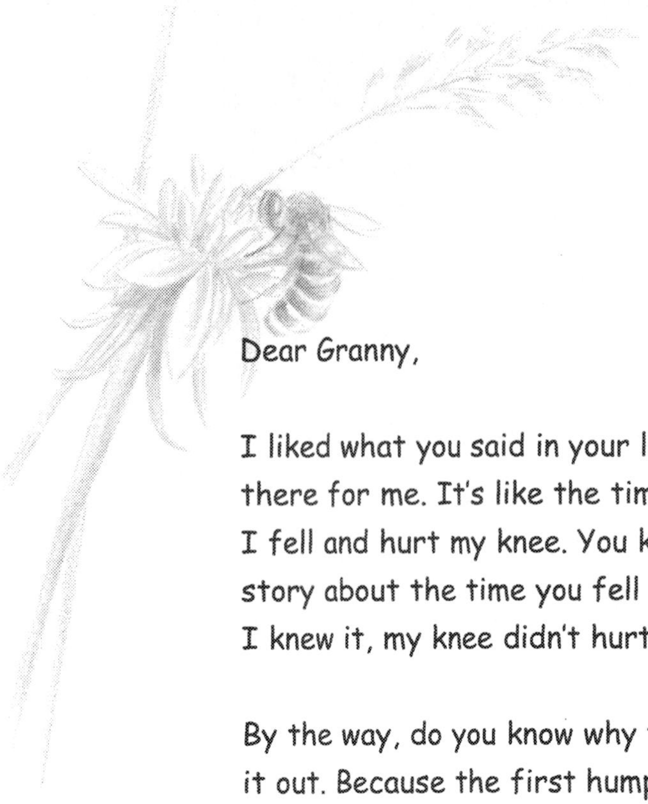

October 2

Dear Granny,

I liked what you said in your letter about listening to me and being there for me. It's like the time when I was around four or five and I fell and hurt my knee. You kissed it, hugged me and told me a story about the time you fell and hurt your elbow — and before I knew it, my knee didn't hurt any more.

By the way, do you know why the camel has two humps? I figured it out. Because the first hump was lonely and wanted a friend.

Do you want to hear some really funny WHYS?

WHY didn't the kids at the beach take a shower?
Answer: Because they were sunbathers.

WHY shouldn't you insult a cat lover?
Answer: Because you'll hurt his felines.

I can't think of any serious WHY questions, but when I do, I'll write you.

Love,
Jordy

P.S. I'm sending you these Why jokes to cheer you up. Mom says you feel depressed having to stay in bed all day, and you need cheering up. And I'm going to keep on sending them until you feel all better.

October 7

Dear Granny,

Why am I not starting with a question? Because I have no question today. I just want to tell you I am sooo happy for you.

Mom says you are <u>all well</u> now and can walk again. You must feel WONDERFUL. Diane and I sent you a box of your favorite chocolate covered pretzels to celebrate.

I hope you have a FANTASTICALLY HAPPY DAY.

LOVE, Jordy

P.S. Why was the moon full? Because it ate too much.

October 12

Dearest Jordy,

Yes, I'm all well again and it's a wonderful, wonderful feeling. I feel alive again. Yesterday, for the first time, I went out without a cane or walker and walked, and walked and walked. It was a glorious feeling – absolutely exhilarating! I felt free, free, free! Excuse the exuberance, but I haven't felt so good since I don't remember when. How does that old saying go, "You don't appreciate what you have until you lose it." I love walking. I always have. It's my favorite form of relaxation. It clears my head and invigorates my spirit.

To further invigorate my spirit, I treated myself to a glass of white wine with chocolate truffles and thoroughly enjoyed the delightful treat.

Tomorrow I'm meeting a friend at the museum. They have a wonderful Cézanne exhibit. I look forward to a leisurely stroll and viewing the beautiful paintings. Next week I'll be going to the Fall Flower Show. I doubt if I'll be able to see all the displays – I still can't walk for too long – but I'll be able to see most of them. Truly, life can be wonderful when you feel well and can walk.

Love,
Granny

October 16

Dear Granny,

I thought of a REALLY serious question. This is it —
Why are kids MEAN?

The worst is when kids call you names. In school yesterday Betsy called Kim "Four Eyes" because she started wearing glasses.

Everybody calls Jim "String bean," but I don't. (He's really skinny). He never says anything but I know he doesn't like it.

During recess Steve called me Fatty. I wanted to punch him. I gave him a dirty look but he just laughed and walked away.

And that's not all. Tom waits until he gets Jake alone at recess and then he punches him. Sometimes when Tom sees me or my friends, he pokes us in the arm or shoulder. Then he says something mean and walks away. I try to stay out of his way. Everyone is afraid of him. Jake told his father and his father told him to stop whining and start fighting back. Jake says he doesn't want to go to school any more, and I don't blame him. I hate mean kids, don't you?

So this is my "Why." Why are kids mean?

Apart from this everything is so-so. School is boring.

Love you, Jordy

P.S. I have another WHY joke that is funny.
WHY did they have a funeral for frog?
Answer: Because he croaked!!!!

"The worst is when kids call you names. In school yesterday Betsy called Kim "Four Eyes" because she started wearing glasses."

October 21

Dear Jordy,

"Why are kids mean?" Hmmm....good question. Let's start with name calling. When I was small and kids teased me, I used to say, "Sticks and stones will break my bones, but names can never hurt me."

That's not true. When kids called me names, it hurt and it made me feel sad. It made me feel angry, and sometimes it even made me feel afraid.

So what can we do when kids call us names?

The first thing to remember is that just because they call you names does not mean it's true. You need to remind yourself that you are a good person, you are a special person, and you won't stoop down to the mean person's level. Usually the best thing to do is just ignore it and walk away. Fighting back can make bullying worse and you can get badly hurt.

Not everyone who calls you names is a bully. Maybe they didn't mean to make you feel bad. If you think the person who hurt your feelings is not really a mean person, you can tell him or her that your feelings were hurt, and why. Say something like: "When you called me names it made me feel bad and I wish you wouldn't do it." It's possible that they didn't mean to hurt your feelings and thought they were only teasing.

> *"Not everyone who calls you names is a bully. Maybe they didn't mean to make you feel bad."*

About Tom punching Jake – that's serious. Bullying gets worse when the bully gets away with it. There are two things Jake can do. The first is to make sure he is not alone in places where Tom usually hits him. This doesn't always work. The best thing for Jake to do is to tell a teacher. Telling a teacher is not tattling. The teacher has a lot of experience in handling these things and can solve the problem without getting Jake into trouble.

Love,
Granny

P.S. How can I be depressed when I have your letters to look forward to and Why jokes to make me laugh. You are so thoughtful, Jordy, and I appreciate it.

October 25

Dear Granny,

WHY are kids mean? You didn't answer my question but I liked what you said even better.

I talked to Jake and he likes your ideas too. He knows that if he lets Tom get away with hitting him, it will get worse. And you know what? — Jake says that he has the feeling that the more Tom sees he's afraid of him, the more Tom enjoys hurting him. But he still tries not to be in the playground when Tom is there.

So please answer my Why question because Jake and I don't really understand why some kids are mean and why Tom always picks on Jake and likes to try to make him cry.

Love you,
Jordy

Why did the zoo get rid of the owl?
Answer: Because he didn't give a hoot.

ELEMENTARY

October 30

Dear Jordy,

I asked Betsy Dorfman, a friend of mine who is a teacher, and she came up with these answers about why kids tease or bully each other.

Sometimes kids are mean because other kids are mean to them. For example, if someone is mean to them at home, they don't feel good about themselves and think that putting someone else down, or calling them names, will make them feel better. Sometimes they are so angry they want to hurt somebody, especially if they have been bullied or physically hurt at home.

Sometimes they are unhappy, sometimes they are jealous, sometimes they want to feel they are better than other kids, and sometimes they want to feel powerful. If the person they pick on shows they're afraid, it makes them feel even more powerful, which is probably why Tom likes picking on Jake. But whatever the reason, bullies need to be stopped. And as a teacher, Betsy feels the best way to stop them is to tell the teacher.

Name calling is something else. Betsy said that the one thing you should NOT do is try to hurt the person back. That will only make things worse. Because sometimes we say and do things that make us ashamed afterwards and sometimes it gets us into real trouble with our parents or teachers.

Betsy also told me how teasing can start as fun but then turn mean and become real bullying. She says that if the person who's being teased acts angry or looks sad, it means the teasing has stopped being fun or friendly, and it is time to stop. If the person who's doing the teasing does not stop, it becomes bullying.

Almost everyone gets teased sometimes – and some of the time it is fun – but when it stops being fun for the person teased it becomes mean.

People sometimes tease people for being different. At other times people want to be part of a group, so even though they may feel they are doing something wrong, they do it because they want to remain part of a group. They might think it will help them fit in with the group, or they might even be afraid of being teased themselves.

Sometimes the teaser does not know when he has stopped being playful and has become hurtful. So it's important to tell them to stop – it's not fun any more.

If the teaser is a mean person, one option is to ignore the teasing and walk away. If they keep on teasing you, speak with a friend, a teacher, or a parent. Talk to someone you trust, tell them what happened and how it makes you feel, and ask them to help you stop it. It's never okay to make a person feel bad on purpose.

These answers seem right to me and I hope you and Jake agree. Please let me know.

In the meantime, I was so happy to receive your letter and thank you again for finding jokes that you think I will find funny.

With much love,
Granny

November 4

Dear Granny,

Why, when you need a hug, do parents give you a lecture?

I had an awful, really AWFUL DAY. I forgot my math homework and got in trouble with the teacher. Then I was the 3rd last person to be picked on the team. I saw Darlene between classes in the hallway and smiled at her. (She's the most popular girl in our class.) She didn't smile back. I felt sick to my stomach.

Why can't I be popular like Darlene? Why can't I be good in sports like Jake? Why can't I be like Diane? (She's so perfect.) Why can't I have a big room like Michael? And I went on and on...just complaining to Mom, nothing more. All Mom had to do was listen or say, "I'm sorry you had a rotten day" and give me a hug. But is that what she did? No, she gave me a lecture on how it's not good to be jealous.

Me, jealous???? Did I say anything when Mom decorated Diane's room and didn't even let me hang up posters in my room? Diane is always Mom's favorite.

Did I say anything when Aunt Fran took Diane to Disneyland and didn't take me? Do I ever say anything when Dad takes Michael to hockey games and never takes me?

Just because I'm the youngest I never get to do anything first. And I never say anything. Is that being jealous?

Anyway, after Mom's long lecture on You Should Not Want To Be Like Other People, she told me I'm good enough exactly the way I am. If I'm good enough exactly the way I am, why won't the popular kids play with me? Why am I one of the last to be picked on the soccer team? And why do I never get anything first in our family? And Mom calls me jealous!!!

Do YOU think I'm jealous, Granny?

Love,
Jordy

P.S. Question:
Why was the gardener jumping up and down?
Answer: Because he had ants in his pants.
(I hope you don't think this is a dirty joke, Granny, but I did think it was funny. Besides, I'm running out of Why jokes.)

November 10

Dear Jordy,

I'm sorry you had a bad day. I wish I were there so I could give you a hug and a kiss, and we could sit and talk about it. You know, Jordy, I shouldn't have favorites, but if I did, it would be you.

Wanting to be like someone else or wanting to have the things they have is not necessarily a bad thing. We all want others to like us and it's a great feeling to be accepted by the popular kids. It hurts when you're not.

"Jealousy is bad when it makes you want to hurt the person you want to be like, or if you are glad when something bad happens to him or her..."

Jealousy is bad when it makes you want to hurt the person you want to be like, or if you are glad when something bad happens to him or her – like if he is an athlete and breaks his leg and you are glad, or if someone has a nicer room than you and you vandalize it, or if you spend your energy hating those who have what you don't have.

That's not you, Jordy. I've known you since you were born, and there's not a mean bone in your body. So if you ask me if you are jealous, I'd say definitely not.

Love you,
Granny

P.S. Did you ever tell your father that you'd like to go to a hockey game? I wouldn't be surprised if he thought maybe you didn't even like hockey.

Love you,
Granny

P.P.S. That's so nice of you to take the time, and to make the effort, to find those Why jokes for me. They do make me smile, and yes, I did find the last one funny. How are you able to find all those jokes? I know they used to have them on bubble gum wrappers, but I don't remember you chewing gum. Do let me know – I'm curious...

November 14

Dear Granny,

Finding Why jokes isn't easy. First I asked Diane and Michael. Michael gave me two good ones. Then Jake, Sarah and I met at recess and we tried to get some Why jokes from the other kids. We got four that way. Then Jake and I went to the library and Mrs. Knapp, the librarian, told us one — the one about why the moon is full. She knew a lot of jokes, but they mostly started with How or What, so that didn't help. Then she showed us how to find some joke books — and those had the best ones. Jake and I wrote them down exactly the way the book said, and now I have six more left that I didn't use. I'm sorry we can't use the WHAT jokes — there are a lot of them and some are really funny, like this one:

What's big, green, lives in New York and has a cold?
Answer: The St-ah-choo of Liberty.

And they have a lot of okay jokes, like: What part of the eye goes to school?
Answer: The pupil.

Those are the only two I remember. I wrote them down to tell Sarah.

What's hard sometimes is to start with a WHY question but if you think about it, you can do it. For example, you could have asked me, Why are you able to get so many Why jokes when they are hard to find? This way you would have followed the Why rule of starting the sentence with why. It's fun when you can do it.

WHY I am still doing it — and will never stop until you tell me to — is because I love you and want to make you laugh — especially now. Mom told me you fell and hurt your ankle. She said I shouldn't worry and it will heal again soon. I feel so sorry for you. How did you hurt it? Does it hurt a lot? You must feel MISERABLE.

You can count on me to keep sending you jokes. Jake says to tell you he is sorry that you got hurt. He says you should have your friends write funny things on your cast — if you have cast. Do you?

This is a long letter and my hand is tired. I started yesterday and finished it today. I love you Granny and will keep the Why jokes coming.

With lots of hugs and kisses, Jordy

P.S. Sometimes Michael tells me WHY jokes to send but YOU wouldn't like them — they are GROSS. Mom says he shouldn't tell them to me but some are really FUNNY.

OOPS! Almost forgot my Why joke—

Why did the fortune teller get all dressed up?
Answer: Because she was going to the CRYSTAL BALL.
(I thought that was a really good one.)

November 18

Dearest Jordy,

"Into one's life some rain must fall,
Some days are dark and dreary."
(By Tennyson, I think)

Yes, there are days when I feel miserable. I hate being confined to home again, I don't like being dependent on other people; I don't like hopping on one foot while trying to get around my kitchen, but I can't put any weight on that ankle. It does look funny, but I don't appreciate the humor and I don't like being dependent on household help again.

When I think back, it was such a stupid accident – not that there is such a thing as an "intelligent" accident. I needed a plate from the top shelf of my kitchen cabinet. Instead of using a small stepladder, I thought I would save a few seconds by standing on a chair. The chair wobbled, and I tried to grab on to the top shelf, but somehow found myself lying on the floor. I was able to crawl to the kitchen table, reach the phone and call for help. I thought I had seriously injured my leg again, but fortunately it turned out to be not-so-serious. You can tell your friend Jake that I don't have a cast, but my ankle is taped up with a special bandage and will be that way for a while.

The doctor says it will take some time before I can walk normally again. However, I will definitely need physical therapy. He recommended – guess who? – my old friend, Sadie Irving,

The Spanish Inquisitor. But I can't complain. This must be my punishment for being stupid – standing on a chair instead of a ladder.

On the positive side, people have been wonderful, especially your family. Your parents sent me crossword puzzles and magazines, Michael sent me a CD, Diane a scrapbook, and I've gotten more boxes of chocolates than I can count – thoughtful gifts to make the time pass quickly – and deliciously. And of course your letters cheer me and some of your Why jokes are – as you say – "really, really, funny."

On the so-so side, well-meaning friends keep phoning me and, while I appreciate their concern, my hearing is still not good and long conversations exhaust me. Aunt Fran offered to come to help, but I graciously declined. Aunt Fran is very sensitive, and she means well, but I prefer the solitary pleasure of silence.

Nothing more to write about, or as they say, "That's all the news for now" or "This too shall pass" or "A stitch in time saves nine." I think I'm feeling feverish again so I'll stop while I'm ahead. I've been receiving a lot of letters that try to make me feel better, but the only ones that ALWAYS work are yours. I always appreciate your taking the time to write. It must be tiring sometimes.

Love you,
Granny

November 22

Dear Jordy,

Life is full of temptations. Sadie, my Spanish Inquisitor, asked if I could write her a letter of recommendation. She is applying for another position. I resisted the temptation to tell her that because she is leaving, I'd be happy to write TWO letters of recommendation. Instead I said, I'll think about it. (One must be polite at all costs – or so they tell me).

That evening, after a hot cup of cocoa and graham crackers, I felt in the mood to write – and I did. I wrote all the things I detested about her, the pain she inflicted upon me, her non-caring attitude – and on and on... highly exaggerated of course, but very satisfying to write. I even wrote something to the effect that she provided me with religious experiences – each time she left, I thanked God. (A little much, but it sounded good when I wrote it.) When I finished, I re-read the letter and gave a satisfied sigh. Aahh.... It expressed exactly how I felt.

Then I crumpled it up into a ball and wrote another letter – this one saying that she was an excellent physical therapist, came highly recommended, was always prompt, never missed a session and while she pushed her patients to their utmost limits, the results were highly gratifying. And I ended with, "I therefore recommend her." This letter was not as satisfying as the first, but it was truthful and she WAS a good physical therapist – I just wish she didn't enjoy her work so much. (I don't think she liked me either).

I must go now. I'm exhausted. Since the accident it seems the less I do the more tired I am. I used to dream about staying in bed for as long as I wanted, just eating chocolates and reading magazines. The dream is much better than the reality.

Complain, complain... it makes me feel better to complain sometimes but I can't let it become a habit.

Love you, and good-night,
Granny

November 27

Dear Jordy,

Today is the first day I was able to go out without a cane or walker. I felt like myself again. It was a great feeling – standing straight instead of leaning forward, not having to use a cane or a walker.

I was in the supermarket and saw Mrs. Knight. Do you remember her? She used to live next door. She's ten years younger than I am and always dressed beautifully.

I almost didn't recognize her. She was bent over her walker – looked older than me – and had that "I'm so tired and it hurts" look that I sometimes saw when I looked in the mirror. She too had an accident and injured her hip. She told me that the prognosis was not good and her recovery was taking much longer than expected. She looked so very tired and discouraged. I felt so very sorry for her – and so very grateful that I was not in the same position.

When I got home I did something I had never expected to do. I sent a beautiful fruit basket to Sadie Irving and a lovely thank-you note in which I expressed my very sincere gratitude. She deserved it. Without her pushing me to do more, I doubt if I would have recovered so quickly. I am truly grateful that I had her as my physical therapist.

Love you,
Granny

December 2

Dear Granny,

Why do parents tell you the same things again and again and again?

CLEAN YOUR ROOM
BRUSH YOUR TEETH
TIE YOUR SHOELACES
EAT YOUR VEGETABLES
COVER YOUR NOSE AND MOUTH WHEN YOU SNEEZE
BEHAVE NICELY
BE POLITE
SAY YOU'RE SORRY
DO YOUR HOMEWORK
DON'T PICK YOUR NOSE
DON'T TALK WITH YOUR MOUTH FULL

They go on and on and on... and even add more things, like "go to sleep on time." They stay up late. Diane stays up late. Michael stays up late. Why do I have to go to sleep when I'm not tired?

What would happen if they stopped telling me what to do? Why do they keep on nagging me even though they know I don't like it?

Love,
Jordy

Why did the cow get a second job?
Answer: Because he needed the MOO-lah.

December 6

Dear Jordy,

You asked a good question in your last letter. But what would happen if parents didn't always tell kids what to do? If you want to write a story, it's a great topic. The title could be: Lucky Me! My parents never told me what to do – and look what happened to me.

Pretend you are writing as a grown up and give situations where you don't do the things they nagged you about... Say you are invited to a big party and you are sitting next to somebody really important. You sneeze right in his face. And this important person talks with his mouth full and you see the cottage cheese and spinach in his mouth. While he's talking, he accidentally spits the spinach and cottage cheese right in your face. The man seated on your left isn't polite and even though you are sitting next to him, he completely ignores you. But you don't mind because you catch him picking his nose (gross!!). Then he gets up, accidentally steps on your toes and even though he could see he hurt you, he doesn't say he's sorry. How does that make you feel about him? And then, in front of everyone, he trips and falls on his face. Doesn't it make you feel glad that his mother didn't nag him about tying his shoelaces?

And then you meet this gorgeous movie star and you are so happy that she stops to talk to you. When she opens her mouth you get a whiff of rancid bad breath. Her mother didn't nag her about brushing her teeth.

And you can go on and on in this vein...

You ask why your parents nag you... I think it's because they care – because they love you. There are different ways of loving a person – some say "I love you" all the time, some give gifts, but the best way parents show they care about you is by doing things for you. They feed you, take care of you, and tell you how to act so that when you grow up you will know how to behave in ways that will not cause you embarrassment. And you'll feel good about yourself because we all know when we do something wrong and feel ashamed when people notice it.

About being told you have to go to sleep when you aren't tired – nobody likes that. But even if you don't feel tired, your body and mind need rest. When you sleep, your body grows and brings you the energy you'll need for the next day. Not getting enough sleep makes it hard for you to concentrate in school, and you don't want that, do you? Especially if your teacher makes you stand up to answer a question and, even if you know the answer, your mind can't concentrate on the answer. It happened to me a couple of times in school because after my parents turned off the light in my room, I waited for about five minutes and then switched it on again. I just <u>had</u> to finish the book I was reading. And of course the next day my mind just didn't work too well.

My mind isn't working so well now, either, because I'm tired and it's late. I've still got a lot of paper work to do – writing thank-you notes, paying bills, etc, etc. My goodness! I just looked at my watch and it is 11:30. That's late! I think I'll leave the paper work until tomorrow and just take time to do a quick crossword puzzle.

Love you,
Granny

December 11

Dear Granny,

Okay, I got the message. Parents tell you what to do because they want you to learn things that won't get you into trouble later on.

But sometimes they tell you to do things just because they want to, and when you ask them why, they say BECAUSE I TOLD YOU SO.

If there was a good reason, I could understand it, but when they say that — <u>that's it</u>!

And I don't get a chance to say what I think. Is that fair? So why do I have to listen to Mom and Dad just because they say so?

Love,
Jordy

"...why do I have to listen to Mom and Dad just because they say so?"

December 15

Dear Jordy,

I don't know if I'm the right person to ask about this because I didn't always listen to my mother, and your mother didn't always listen to what I told her when she was a child. But you asked a valid question, and I'll try to answer.

I think one reason to listen to your mother is it saves a lot of angry confrontations that seldom resolve things to everyone's satisfaction. And while you are living in your parents' home and getting food, clothing, toys, and an allowance from them, they feel you should follow their rules. Sometimes they have a good reason for telling you what to do but are too tired to explain if the reason is long – or if a child keeps arguing with them – so it's easier to stop the argument by saying "Because I said so." It may not be fair, but that's the way it is and sometimes it's better not to argue.

As to why you have to listen to your mother and father – it's because they are your parents. They are the ones who love you and spend their time and money to raise you. They make mistakes sometimes, but they do their best. When they are tired, they don't always do or say the right thing, but even if you think they are not fair, it's better to listen to them. They are human, they make mistakes, but they love you and want the best for you. They are your parents and deserve your respect.

You don't always have to like it, but that's the way it is.

The thing to remember when they are unreasonable is that they do love you and they try their best, but they are human – which is another way of saying they are not perfect. But then again, neither are we.

I don't know if this answer will satisfy you, but it's what I believe.

Love you,
Granny

JORDY

December 19

Dear Granny,

Why are Jake and me singing this song?
"No more homework, no more books,
No more teachers' dirty looks."

Because winter vacation will start next week and all of us are going away somewhere. Dad's taking us to Disney World for a couple of days. Jake will be visiting his aunt in London. Sarah will be going to stay with her cousins in New York.

I'll send you postcards from Disney World.

Love,
Jordy

December 23

Dear Jordy,

Have a wonderful, wonderful holiday. I can't wait to hear all about it. Phone me when you get back home. My telephone now has an extra loud attachment so it's easier for me to hear phone conversations.

I'm so glad you're going to have a special holiday. Enjoy, enjoy, and bring back many happy memories. I look forward to getting your postcards.

Love,
Granny

January 3

Dear Granny,

Why am I writing you today? To tell you the funniest story. It's true. My friend Sarah told it to me, and we laughed so hard that Sarah almost peed in her pants.

You know Sarah's sister Ellie? She's three years old and a spoiled brat, but that's beside the point. This is about how Ellie hates their new baby. Nobody pays any attention to Ellie any more. The baby gets tons of presents and she gets none. So Ellie kept asking her mother again and again to give the baby back and her mother kept telling her again and again that she can't and won't give the baby back. Finally Ellie got the message. She went to her mother and asked, Can we take her to a forest?

Sarah and I laughed and laughed. Sarah says she doesn't blame Ellie because the baby is a pain in the neck. She cries all night and wakes everybody up. But she's sorry for Ellie and bought her a giant pink lollipop in the shape of a heart.

At dinner Daddy told the funniest story about his day at the office. Everyone was laughing so hard. Do you have any funny stories? Michael tells good ones but Mom says they are not in good taste.

Love you,
Jordy

January 8

Jordy dear,

I'm concerned! Your mother tells me that you haven't been sleeping well lately, that you woke up a few times with nightmares, and "you are not acting yourself" – whatever that means.

Can you tell me if there is anything troubling you? Is anyone teasing you at school? Are you overwhelmed with homework and the tests coming up? Did something happen at school that was unpleasant or frightened you?

Please tell me, Jordy, because I am deeply troubled and don't want to spend the nights tossing and turning, unable to sleep because I am worried about you.

Do telephone me very, very soon. Never mind that I can't hear that well – I can turn the volume up on the phone.

I'm waiting on pins and needles (how can a person wait on pins and needles?) but that somehow expresses how I feel.

Anxiously awaiting your call,
Love,
Granny

January 13

Dear Granny,

Why do parents fight about money?

A friend of mine needs to know. My friend has very nice parents but she has to know what to do about something that is going on.

My friend's parents have started fighting about money and it scares her. They raise their voices and sound so angry that it makes her stomach turn. Once she tried to go in the room where they were fighting to try to get them to make peace but they yelled at her to leave. She left — fast.

My friend is worried that if they keep on fighting they will get divorced. Nancy — a girl in my class — her parents are divorced and they used to fight a lot; Jake's parents fight a lot too and Freddy said they are going to get divorced. I am worried that my friend's parents will get divorced too.

What do you think? Please answer right away so I can tell my friend what to do.

Love you,
Jordy

P.S. Remember when I said I wanted to be an astronaut? Well, now I decided I want to be a millionaire so I won't ever have to fight about money.

January 18

Dear Jordy,

Money is important because one needs money to buy food, clothing, pay the rent, pay medical bills, school expenses, etc. And because it's important, people take the subject seriously, and if money becomes scarce, people get scared and fight about it.

When the economy is bad, people are frightened. Many are afraid they may lose their jobs. Even if their jobs are safe, some believe the economy will get worse and they don't want to spend money unnecessarily. This can lead to fights between husbands and wives about where and how their money will be spent. Sometimes the wife thinks money should be spent one way and the husband thinks it should not be spent that way – which leads to fights. Because the subject is important, it gets very emotional.

Fights can be loud, and people say things that they don't really mean. Parents, like children, say things during fights and then make up, become friends again, and forget what they said. But the children who hear the fight <u>don't</u> forget, and it scares them and sometimes makes them think their parents will divorce.

Tell your friend to leave the room when her parents fight because fights between parents are private and should NOT be overheard by others.

"When the economy is bad, people are frightened. ...they don't want to spend money unnecessarily. This can lead to fights between husbands and wives."

If they fight in front of her, she should tell them clearly that their fighting scares her. I'm sure her parents don't want to frighten her and will not fight about money matters any more in her presence.

You are very lucky, Jordy, that your parents love each other very, very much and will not divorce even if they should ever fight about money. Your parents went through many difficult times together and even if they argued at times, in the end it made them stronger and more committed to their marriage.

If someone still has a problem with her parents fighting, or if it becomes more frequent, please let me know. I feel confident that you and I can come up with some good solutions. I plan to come to visit you and if these problems get worse, I can be there to help you solve them.

Love,
Granny

January 22

Dear Granny,

WHY am I the happiest person in the whole world?

I'll tell you. It started when Darlene, the MOST POPULAR girl in our class talked to me at recess. Darlene, Ashley and Steve stick together and everyone wants to be friends with them. Darlene said maybe we could do our homework together and invited me to her house. Her parents are divorced and she lives with her mother and stepfather. We had a really, really nice time, and then I asked her to do homework at my house.

On Wednesday she came over, we did our homework, and she stayed for supper. Darlene said Mom's chocolate chip cookies were the best she ever tasted. She said she wished she had a sister and brother like Diane and Michael. I told her about you, Granny, and she said she would help me find WHY jokes to send to you. I can't believe it, but I think she wants to be friends.

Tomorrow I'm bringing her a bag of Mom's chocolate chip cookies and maybe we'll share them at recess.

Love,
Jordy

Question:
Why was the calendar never home on weekends?
Answer: Because it had a lot of DATES.

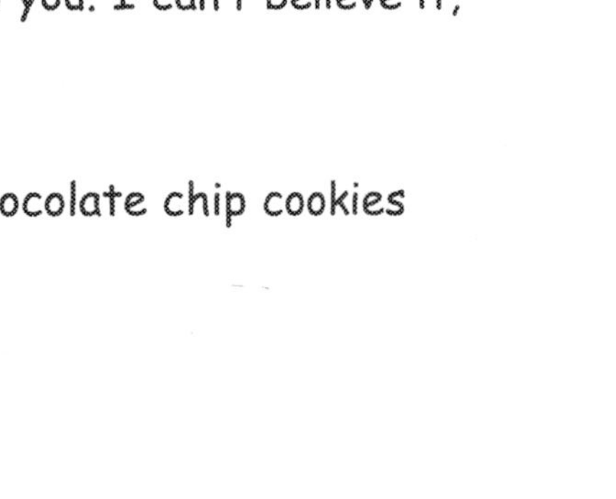

January 26

Dear Jordy,

I'm so happy you have a new friend. Enjoy your friend; enjoy school. Again, I am so glad for you.

I'm sorry this is such a short letter, but it's late and I'm having trouble keeping my eyes open!

Love,
Granny

P.S. I almost forgot – I heard a Why joke on a
TV cooking show the other day:
Why do potatoes make good detectives?
Because they keep their eyes peeled.

February 2

Dear Granny,

School is great.

Darlene is always at our house after school and we do our homework. (Mom helps us sometimes.) Sometimes Darlene even stays for supper. I bring chocolate chip cookies to school every day now, and sometimes Darlene stays with me for recess and sometimes I share them with Steve and Ashley too.

Yesterday Mom said she thinks Darlene is lonely. Isn't that CRAZY!! Darlene, who is so cool and who everyone is dying to be best friends with. I told Darlene what Mom said. I thought she would laugh, but she just gave me a funny look and didn't say anything. I hope I didn't insult her. I wish Mom wouldn't have said anything. I don't want anything to spoil our friendship. Tomorrow I think I'll bring brownies to school.

Love,
Jordy

P.S. Why do worms go to the library?
Answer: To look for book worms.

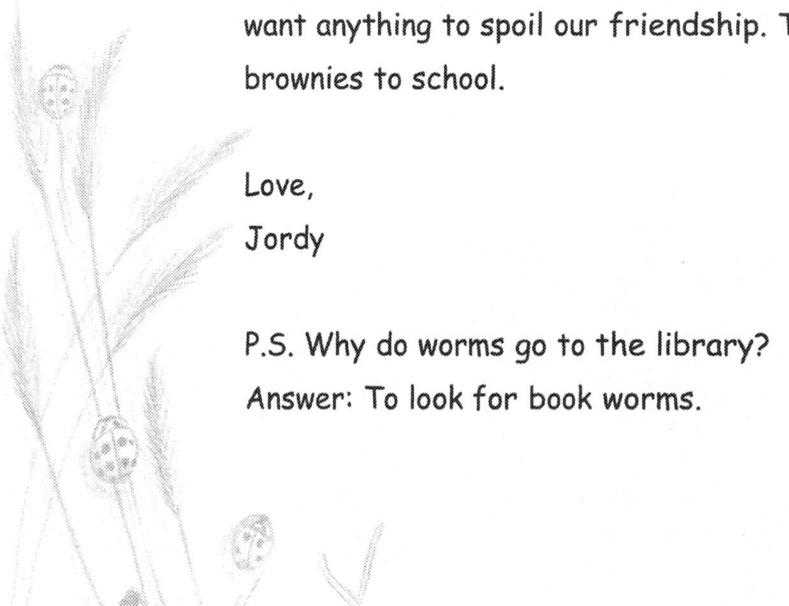

February 8

Dear Granny,

WHY do people try to make you feel bad when you're feeling good?

Sarah is mad at me because she said I like Darlene better than her. She said Darlene is only friends with me because I help her with her homework. That's just not true! She helps me with math and I help her with English and a few other subjects.

As if that isn't enough, Mom says I shouldn't bribe Darlene by bringing her cookies and stuff. Just because I asked Mom to make her special jelly roll to take to school, she started with one of her "You are a very special person" lecture — "You are smart, loyal, blah, blah, blah... and Darlene is lucky to have a friend like you." Sometimes mothers don't understand anything.

On top of that she made me feel bad by asking why I don't have Sarah join us at recess. Doesn't she know I already thought of that! I CAN'T ask Sarah to be with Darlene, Steve, Ashley and me because if I do Darlene and her friends might not want me to be friends with them too. I know Sarah feels sad about it, and I feel bad about it too, but when I become real, real, really good friends with them I'll ask them all to come to my house and I'll invite Sarah too.

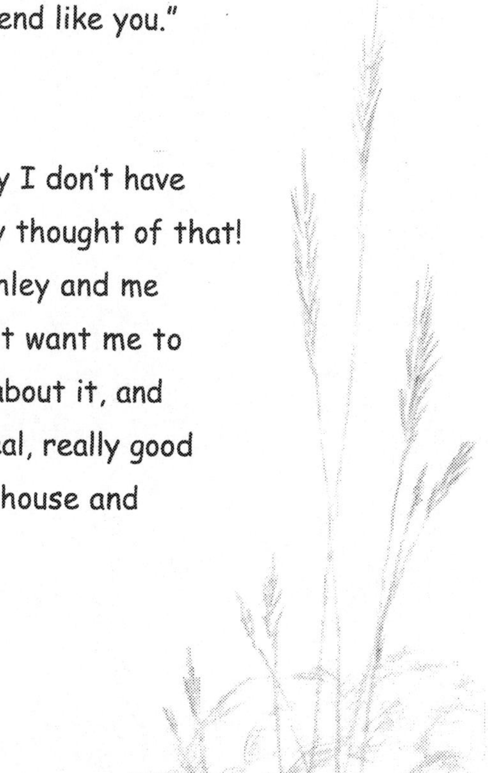

Jake didn't say anything but he doesn't come over to talk to me at recess any more. Maybe he's mad because I don't do homework with him anymore.

Why won't my family let me be happy? Even Diane and Michael ask me why I don't phone Sarah any more. I don't phone her because when I talk about Darlene she gets upset and somehow there's nothing else to talk about now.

When I invite Sarah and Darlene to my house, Sarah won't be angry at me any more and we'll all be friends. I KNOW Darlene will love Sarah once she gets to know her and even though Steve and Ashley don't like Sarah, I don't care. Darlene will like her and we'll all be friends — the three of us — and Jake too of course.

Love,
Jordy

Why did the ghoul want to leave summer camp?
Answer: Because he missed his mummy.

February 13

Dear Granny,

WHY do people say things to hurt you? Why?

I'm so angry I could scream!!

On Monday I brought Darlene some of Mom's almond chocolate bars after school. And when we were sharing, Darlene said to me, "Jordy, you shouldn't really be eating so many sweets. They'll make you even MORE fat. Don't you want to lose weight?"

I thought I would DIE. My heart went to my stomach and I thought I would fall down. I tried not to cry but the tears wouldn't stop. Darlene tried to stop me but I ran straight home. I didn't go back to school for two days. Mom couldn't make me go.

Sarah was right. Darlene never liked me. She was just friends because I helped her with her homework. I even did her English composition for her. That's why she said she liked me. Mom said Darlene didn't mean anything bad but I don't care. I'm sorry I didn't hurt her like she hurt me. When she told me her stepfather didn't like her, I should have said I don't blame him. I never want to see her as long as I live!

I miss you Granny, I wish you were here.

Love,
Jordy

February 17

Dear Jordy,

I wish I was with you too.

In answer to your question, we all hurt each other sometimes, even if we don't mean to. I think it's because we care and when we care we want to help, even when the other person doesn't want help. Do you remember some times when this happened?

Do you remember the time when I was smoking and you gave me that big lecture on why I had to stop? And when you saw I wouldn't listen and wouldn't give up cigarettes, you got up at night and threw away my package of cigarettes. Do you think I liked that?

Do you remember the time I took a second piece of cake at your birthday party and the look I gave your mother when she told me I didn't need that second piece? Do you remember the tone of voice I used when I answered her?

And remember the time when Diane overheard your mother and father saying that it was dangerous for Aunt Lily to drive. Diane didn't say anything but when no one was looking she went to Aunt Lily's purse, took out her car keys, and threw them in the incinerator. Aunt Lily didn't speak with Diane for weeks and your mother had to have the repair man over to fix the incinerator. Do you remember what your father said to Diane when he got the bill?

I'm sorry Darlene hurt your feelings. I hope when you get over feeling angry you can forgive her.

I'm sorry I'm not with you. I wish I could give you a hug.

Love,
Granny

"...we all hurt each other sometimes, even if we don't mean to. I think it's because we care and when we care we want to help, even when the other person doesn't want help."

JORDY

Dear Granny, February 22

Why do feelings change so much?

Yesterday at school Darlene tried to apologize but I didn't let her finish. I walked straight past her. I still hate her and never want to see her again. I can't believe there was a time I would have given anything to be her friend. Do you remember the time she first smiled at me and I was the happiest person in the world? How could feelings change so much?

Sarah is still my friend but it's not the same. I think she's still angry at me. Jake and I still get along okay and we play ball at recess sometimes, which is sort of fun, but I don't enjoy it as much any more.

I wish school was over and I could visit with you.

Love, Jordy

February 26

Dear Jordy,

I am so very, very sorry you are going through such a difficult time. I wish there was something I could say that would make things better, but I don't have the words. I too wish we could be together. When is your next school holiday? If it's a long weekend, perhaps you could come to visit me? I'm sure I could persuade your parents to let you come.

Love you, and hoping to see you soon,
Granny

March 3

Dear Granny,

WHY did this happen?

I decided to lose weight and show Darlene that I could be as thin as her. Each day I gave away my lunch and only had a diet coke and chips. I'm hungry all the time. When I get home I eat two hard boiled eggs with milk and it fills me up. For supper I tell Mom I'm not hungry, but at night I can't sleep because I'm so hungry so sometimes I get up and take two pieces of cake and milk and then I fall asleep right away.

This morning I stepped on the scale. I was sure I lost at least five pounds. I looked down and saw I had GAINED TWO POUNDS.

Why? How could this happen? I was eating practically nothing for four whole days.

I feel sick when I think about it. If I'm going to gain weight when I eat practically nothing then I might as well eat all I want. Do you have an answer — not that I think I want to hear it.

Love,
Your miserable grandchild,
Jordy

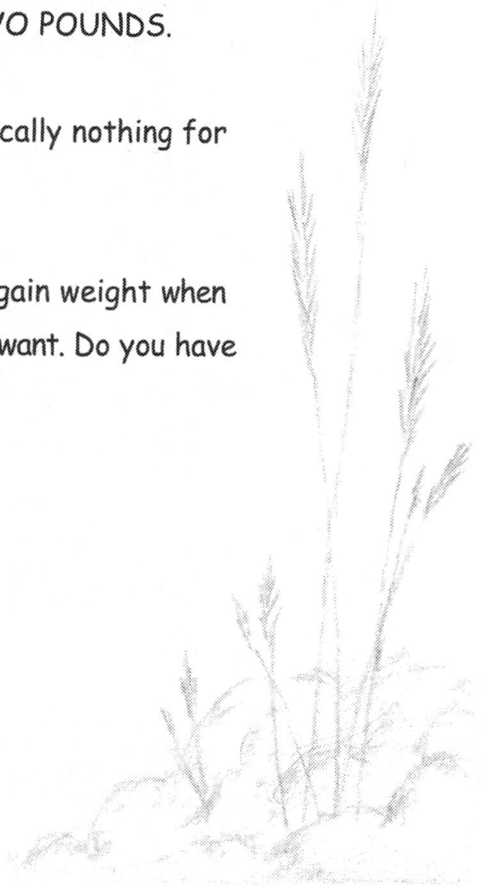

March 8

Dear Jordy,

I'm so sorry. You tried so hard – only to gain weight. It's not uncommon though. My next door neighbor, Nancy Heller, is a nutritionist. She says that it's not unusual for people to gain weight if they eat too little. The reason is that the body will react as if it has survived a famine and will store fat to protect it from future food storages. That could be why you gained weight, instead of losing weight.

Nancy said that children's bodies come in different sizes and shapes and some are a little heavier than others. She's very much against children who are slightly overweight going on diets because kids are still growing and have important nutritional needs.

But if you still want to be slimmer, the way to do it, she says, is to watch less TV, be more active (like walking, swimming, riding a bike) and ask your mother to prepare healthy low-fat foods as well as lots of fresh fruit and vegetables. And she said to make sure that you are allowed to have a small piece of cake or a cookie two or three times a week. In addition, you can have any meal you like, your absolute favorite meal, one day a week. I'm sure your mother won't mind making it for you. The portion sizes will have to be smaller – enough to make you feel satisfied but not so much that you will feel stuffed. Is that okay with you?

Your mom told me she took you to your doctor and he said you will lose your weight or grow into it, eventually. So apart from making some changes in your food intake, you don't really have to worry about your weight.

Nancy said that the kids she is REALLY sorry for are the very thin kids who are anorexic. They have real problems. Some kids are so afraid of gaining weight that they vomit after eating a normal meal. Some get so sick that they have to be hospitalized, and some even die. So Jordy, you are really lucky that you don't have that problem.

By the way, Jordy, who is the most popular relative in our family? That's a no-brainer. Uncle Joe, of course. And is he thin? No way! Would you want to see him thin like Uncle Henry, who is mean and cross all the time? Think about it. Would you like Uncle Joe any better if he were thinner?

Love,
Granny

P.S. Nancy also said that maybe you have too much stress with all the homework you are doing, and that stress and lack of sleep can make the body retain fat. Also, your mother lets you play video games at night to help you relax, but maybe you need sleep instead. It's something you might want to think about and discuss with your mother.

P.P.S. I miss the WHY jokes.

March 13

Dear Granny,

Why are people nice when you want to keep on hating them? Here is a copy of the e-mail Darlene sent me.

"I didn't mean to hurt you. I thought I was helping you by giving you good advice. I'm sorry we are not friends any more. I miss going to your house. I always wanted to have a home with a mother, a father, a sister and a brother like your family. You are very lucky. I liked coming over to your house and pretending I was part of your family. I understand your being mad at me and I'm sorry. Do you think we can be friends again?"

I'm not mad at Darlene any more, and we still hang around at recess sometimes, but I'm not comfortable around her any more and I think she's not comfortable with me. Mom says in time we will be like we were before. Maybe. Jake and I are good friends again. We're both competing in the spelling bee and we're both in the school band. We hate the same teachers and we both have the same favorite teacher, Miss Perkins. We have a lot to talk about and somehow Darlene is not so important to me any more.

Love,
Jordy

P.S. I'm sorry I haven't sent you Why jokes in a while, but here's a good one. Jake got it for me.

Question: Why shouldn't you tell a pig your secrets?
Answer: Because he'll squeal.

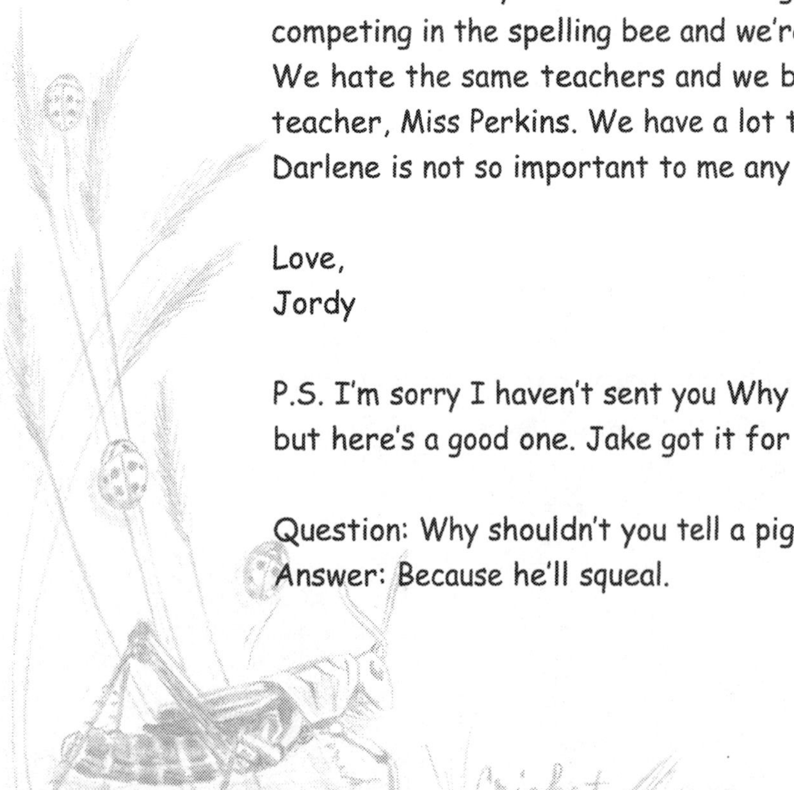

March 19

Dear Granny,

Why do teachers give so much homework? Why? Why?

My shoulders are killing me. Mom weighed my backpack and she said it weighed 43 pounds but it feels like at least 100. You should see all the books I have to bring home every day for homework. Granny — I hate homework. Mom says I can't go outside with my friends until it's all done. She won't even let me watch any videos or TV. It's been raining for days and days and finally it's sunny outside. I want so badly to go out but I can't because by the time I get finished with all the homework it will be dark. Do you think that's fair? I don't!!! Did you have to do hours and hours of homework when you went to school? All I want to do is go outside or watch TV. HELP ME!!!

Love,
Jordy

Question: Why can't you come to my house to play video games after school?
Answer: Because I have to help my Dad with my homework. (I wish! Mom helps me sometimes, but she makes me do almost all of it myself.)

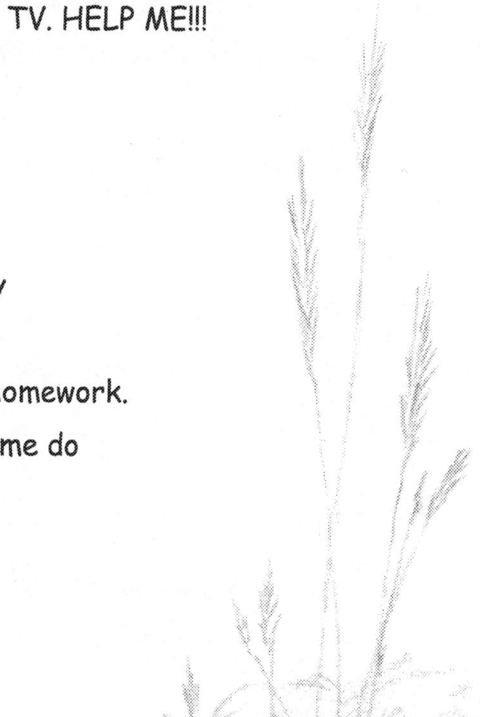

March 24

Dear Jordy,

When I hear your homework problem, I find myself humming one of my favorite songs – "I'm glad I'm not young any more." Do you remember that song? It's from the video we watched at Aunt Fran's house – "GIGI" – and Maurice Chevalier sang it.

To answer your questions, no, I didn't have much homework when I was your age; and no, I don't think so much homework is fair, but that's not relevant to your problem. You need a solution.

I'd suggest that you meet with your teacher to discuss the problem. Be sure to take a pencil and notebook to write down the points to remember; otherwise it's easy to forget. Listen to what she has to say, and then mention some things that might be helpful – such as having a homework assignment book to better time manage your homework or using notecards and outlines.

Then talk to your mother about the meeting, show her the solutions you and the teacher came up with, and ask her to help you schedule time for playing games or relaxing with your friends. I think you have an excellent chance of getting the play time you want. I wouldn't push the TV or video watching because I don't think your mother will give in about this.

Good luck and I hope this will help resolve the homework problem. Let me know how it works out.

With much love,
Granny

March 29

Dear Granny,

WHY does a person embrace change? Because they are ready.

How do I know? I heard Mom telling Aunt Fran she wants to bake cakes and sell them to stores. Aunt Fran didn't think it was a good idea and tried to talk her out of it, but Mom said she was ready to "Embrace Change." Isn't that a neat expression? I could just imagine Mom hugging this ghostly figure wrapped in white sheets, with the sign Embrace Change on him.

I think Mom should do it — she's makes THE best cookies and cakes and brownies. Daddy said that with the economy the way it is, it's not a bad idea to have an extra income. Then Mom started to say something, but then she saw me and asked me to go watch TV. Money talk is a scary thing and I wasn't sorry to leave.

I have tons of homework and have to go now.

I love you and will write again real soon.

Love,
Jordy

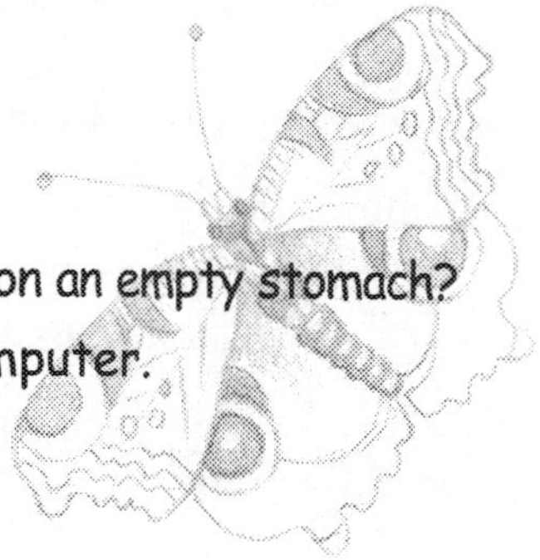

P.S. Question: Why shouldn't you do homework on an empty stomach?
Answer: Because it's better to do it on a computer.

JORDY

April 2

Dear Granny,

Why do I have to be the youngest in the family?

It's awful to be the youngest. I never get to do anything. Michael and Diane get to watch TV at night and even though I begged and begged to see the movie — It was a Harry Potter movie and I was DYING to see it — but Dad said it would end past my bedtime so I missed it. I can't even complain because nobody wants to listen.

I always have to miss things. I always get the hand-me-downs. I got Michael's old beat-up bike when he got a new one.

All my teachers had Diane in their classes so they always expect me to be perfect like her. Is that fair? Mom says I'm not Diane and Diane's not me, but you try telling the teachers that.

Everyone — Mom, Dad, Michael, Diane — all boss me around. And if I tell them what to do, I get into trouble. Diane has a boyfriend and all she does is talk and talk and talk to him over the phone. When she's not talking to him she's talking to her friends ABOUT him. So I figured I would tell her what to do. I told her she was acting stupid and to stop talking about her boyfriend this and her boyfriend that. I mean, enough is enough is enough!!!

You think Diane is perfect? Well, she's not. You should have heard how she yelled at me. And who got in trouble? Me. Mom made me go to my room for teasing Diane about her boyfriend, and if I do it again I'll be grounded for two days.

I wish I was the oldest. You were the oldest. What was it like?

Love,
Jordy

April 5

Dear Jordy,

I hated being the oldest of four. I was the first child and my parents expected me to be perfect. If I made any mistakes or did not do well in school, they sat me down for long talks about why I should do better. My mother believed that if the first child was well behaved and listened to her parents, she would set an example for the siblings and they would follow suit.

Can you imagine what it was like to always have to be perfect, with parents having so many expectations? I always felt the other kids were allowed to do things I was never allowed to do. The one who was the most spoiled – who never had to follow most of the rules – was the youngest. We all thought she was the favorite, and none of us thought it was fair.

As for getting hand-me-downs, Michael had to work for the money to pay for half his bike, so perhaps he feels it isn't fair that you got his old one "for nothing." Did you ever ask Michael how he feels about being the middle child? Dozens of books have been written about the difficulties of being a middle child, and I think Michael could relate to many of those things.

Every child seems to want something they don't have – the youngest wants the privileges one gets when one is older, and the oldest envies the youngest's lack of responsibilities. And if one is the only child, he or she wants to have at least one sister or brother.

Even grown-ups are that way sometimes. When they are young and poor they want to be rich and if they spend their lives struggling to be rich and finally make it, they talk about the happiest days of their lives when they were young, poor, and struggling. Life can be funny.

I'm digressing, I know, but your letter made me think, and remember the time when I was in elementary school and bitterly complained about my teachers. They were extremely strict and often unfair. When I complained to my mother, she told me to stop complaining because I was lucky to be able to attend school at all. My parents were immigrants and felt school was a privilege. Therefore all my complaints about school were disregarded. They always sided with the teacher, even when she was wrong. So I learned not to complain to my parents.

When I became a mother, my responses to your mother's complaints were nuggets of wisdom such as "Stop complaining. Do something about it." They did not elicit words of gratitude. As I recall, the words she used were definitely not words of appreciation. But she did learn not to complain to me.

"The great advantage of a journal is that it's private. Nobody will see it, nobody will get mad, nobody will give you advice and nobody will tell you to stop complaining."

So, as you're in the third generation of CAN'T COMPLAINERS, I would like to suggest the following: Start a Complaint Journal. It can be such fun. Imagine writing down every single thing you think is unfair. Don't stint – have a good time expressing all your feelings. The great advantage of a journal is that it's private. Nobody will see it, nobody will get mad, nobody will give you advice and nobody will tell you to stop complaining.

Try it Jordy. It's a lovely feeling to complain to your heart's desire without anyone stopping you.

My, such a long letter. My hand is cramped and I feel I've written much too much, but I'm too tired to re-read it so I will send it off with my fondest good wishes, a hug and a kiss.

Love you so much,
Granny

Complaint Journal
Why me? Why, why, why?
Why do I have
to be the youngest? I never
get to do anything. I always
have to miss things. Is that
fair? I mean, enough is
enough... And who got into
trouble? me...

April 8

Dear Granny,

Why do I like to write you?
Because it makes me feel good.
To-night I am thinking of you Granny.
I miss you, at night especially.

I miss cuddling next to you on the sofa,
I miss you making me laugh.
I miss you telling me stories.
You tell the funniest stories.
Nobody tells stories like you.

At night sometimes I want to be a baby again,
And have you kiss me and tuck me into bed.
I miss talking to you at night.

That's why I write you.
Because at night I talk to you
when I write you letters.
And even if it's late at night
And Mom sees my light on
If she sees I'm writing,
She knows it's to you
And she doesn't say anything.

It doesn't matter if I'm tired
Because I can finish the letter another night.
But it's still not the same as you being here.
I wish you would come to visit.

I wish you lived here again
And you could tuck me into bed at night
And make me laugh.

In the day time I'm okay
It's just at night that I'm lonely sometimes
And I think of you,
And I write.

Do you miss me too?

I love you,
Jordy

April 11

Dearest Jordy,

I miss you too, my darling. Any time you feel really, really lonely, tell me and I will come to be with you.

In the meantime, writing letters make you feel better and receiving them makes me happy.

It's interesting that you say you sometimes wish you were a baby. Interesting because your mother often tells me that she is sorry you are not a baby any more – she loved cuddling you but says you get embarrassed when she does it now that you're older. Maybe because it's during the day, when your friends are there.

The best time to cuddle and talk is at night. I remember your mother was not a talkative child, but at night I would tuck her in bed, cuddle, and we would talk. We had such nice, nice talks.

Wouldn't it be nice if you told your mother that you sometimes feel lonely at night and miss cuddling? This way she would come to your room, sit on your bed, and you could tell her what you are thinking. You could even ask her about the talks she had with me when she was your age. Ask her to tell you the story about the time the dog barked at night and what happened afterwards.

I love you very much, Jordy, and can't wait for summer vacation when we can be together again.

Love,
Granny

April 14

Dear Granny,

Freddy, a kid in my class, came over to me at lunch and told me that Jake's parents are getting divorced for sure. Freddy's such a liar. I don't believe him, but sometimes he tells the truth, so you never know. He asked Sarah if she liked Steve. She said yes, and now he's telling everybody that Sarah has a boyfriend. Sarah didn't mean it that way. But Freddy told everyone and now Sarah is embarrassed when she sees Steve and doesn't want to go to school. He told Darlene that Steve's father lost his job, and I think it's true but Steve said it's not.

Mom says I shouldn't listen to Freddy because he "mixes truth with fiction" and is a troublemaker. I told her if I don't talk to him he might get mad and tell stories about me. Mom said be polite to him but say I have something to do — and then walk away. Sometimes Mom comes up with good ideas.

Jake is always in a bad mood now. He told me that the "Rule of Three" worked in his exams. He thinks things happen in threes. He failed two exams in a row and said he KNEW he would fail the third — and it was true. He failed in History. Dad said if he was less superstitious and studied more, he would get better marks.

That's all the news for now,
Love you lots and lots and lots,
Jordy

JORDY

April 19

Dear Granny,

Why do grown-ups say it's "for your own good" when they snoop? But if I snoop, it's "not respecting a person's privacy" — which is what Mom told me when I peeked in Diane's diary a few months ago.

Here's a story Diane told me about parents snooping — Diane's best friend Marcy keeps a diary and writes down EVERYTHING — including what she thinks about her parents when they are mean to her. Well, Marcy's mother went into her room when Marcy was in school and read everything Marcy wrote in her diary. Her mother told her father and they both sat her down and said they wanted to "communicate." Communicate meant that they were mad at her because she wrote mean things about them. They said they all have to go to a counselor to learn how to "communicate better." Diane told me that Marcy cried when she told Diane about this. Marcy said she couldn't trust them for one minute. She wouldn't be surprised if they go through her backpack too, and maybe even check her cell phone to read her text messages about her new boyfriend and how gorgeous he is.

I thought that was a dirty thing for her parents to do — to snoop and embarrass her. What do you think? Her parents said they only wanted to protect her, but Diane says the ones Marcy needs protection from is them.

You always see the parents' side of things, Granny, but how can you explain this? No matter which way you look at it, snooping is WRONG. Tell me what YOU think. Diane thinks they are hypocrites.

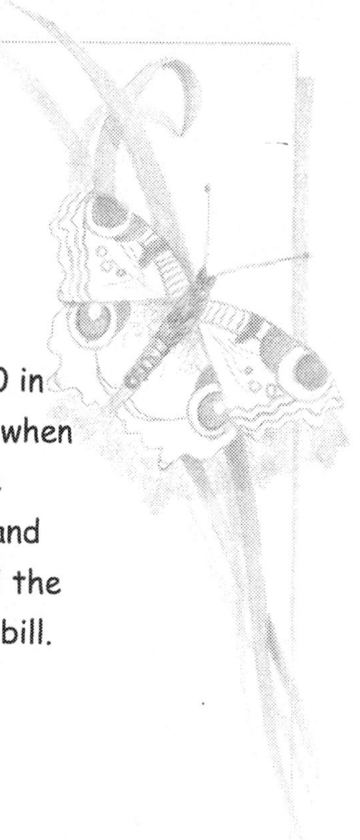

Nothing much doing in school. Still lots of homework. I got 100 in spelling and Mom took me out for ice-cream. Mom is more fun when she is outside the house than when she is inside and telling me what to do. Mom told me a really funny story about when you and her went to a restaurant and found a dead fly in the salad and the waiter thought you were making it up to get out of paying the bill.

X♡X♡X♡X
Jordy

P.S. Why did the two men get into a fight with the clock?
Answer: Because the clock struck one.

(It takes a minute to get this joke, but if you think about it, you'll get it.) I'm running low on jokes. Michael promised me a couple but you know how HIS jokes are (a <u>tiny</u> bit dirty) — so I can't send them. Dad says they're racy — I say they're a bit dirty. I'll be going to the library next week to pick up some videos and will find some WHY jokes there.

"You always see the parents' side of things, Granny...No matter which way you look at it, snooping is WRONG."

April 22

Dear Jordy,

Parents are in a difficult position, Jordy, when they think something dangerous could happen to their child, so they may react by behaving in a way that is not always right, like looking in a private diary.

I was at a luncheon a few weeks ago. Eight women sat at our table: six women about my age and the other two around your mother's age. We were talking about the dangers facing children and teenagers in today's society. The grandmothers were especially worried. Their general opinion was that everything possible should be done to make sure kids are not involved in drugs, exposed to the dangers of the Internet, etc. etc. None of them believed it was right to snoop, but each felt that the child must be protected, even if it meant snooping.

The two younger mothers were more relaxed about possible dangers. One said she carpools her kids to and from school, hears what they talk about (they forget she is there listening) and she has no concerns. She said they were good kids and she has no reason to worry. The other mother said she does not go through her kids' diaries, but she does monitor their Internet use. She calls it monitoring, not spying. She also reads their texts and every once in a while catches them doing something she doesn't approve of. But as long as it's not serious, she ignores it and says nothing to them about it. The reason she monitors, she says, is that she likes to sleep at night without worrying.

These situations are not only about spying or snooping. They are also about trust. I know parents need to earn their child's trust and that routine spying on their kids, when they have no reason to suspect something's wrong, isn't showing much trust in them.

But the problem I have is that even if they trust their kids, parents don't necessarily trust the strangers who enter their homes via the Internet. How can parents protect kids if they don't know who these strangers are and what they're saying or doing?

I must confess, Jordy, that as a parent and grandparent I feel it is our responsibility to protect children from harm. And if that means stooping so low as to spy on them, I would probably do it. However, I would tell them about it beforehand and explain why I felt it necessary to snoop.

I know this is not the answer you want, Jordy. I know it's not right to read another person's diary or to invade their privacy – but if my child or grandchild were in danger, I would do everything possible to protect them.

Please write and tell me what you think. I hope you are not too disappointed in me.

Love you,
Granny

April 24

Dear Granny,

After I wrote to you, Mom, Dad, Michael, Diane and me were eating supper and we talked about Marcy's mother sneaking into her room and reading her diary. Diane said that her ex-boyfriend — the one who dumped her — got a speeding ticket a week after he got his driver's license. He told his parents, they gave him a lecture, and he thought it was over. Then when he was cleaning out the car, he found a hidden computer tracking device to check up on him. He was so MAD. He told his parents and they said they were worried about him and only did it to protect him. He yelled at them and told them what he thought about them. For that his parents took away his car keys and grounded him for two weeks.

Michael said he didn't blame Diane's ex. He said if Mom and Dad did that to him, he would <u>really</u> give them something to worry about.

Mom and Dad let us all talk and say what we wanted. Diane wanted to know the difference between a parent who likes to control and a parent who wants to protect. Michael wanted to know if a hypocrite is someone who says one thing and does something else.

When we all finished saying what we thought, Mom said she had gotten together with other mothers and they had decided on what to do if they were worried about their kids getting into trouble. IF, and only IF, they think their kid is looking at forbidden

Web sites or sending or receiving bad messages, they will check their kid's messages. BUT — and this is the big BUT — they will tell their kid about what they are doing and if they see that he or she is not doing anything wrong, they will stop. They would not put a computer device in the car UNLESS they knew he was drag racing or doing something dangerous like that. Daddy kept saying "You gotta do what you gotta do" — so I never figured out whose side he was on.

The talking went on and on. I got bored and went upstairs to watch TV. There's one thing I know for sure. If I ever get a diary I'll make sure there is a lock on it. What's private is private and even if there is a good reason, I don't ever want someone going through my personal things. But I really don't need a diary, Granny — because I have you!

I'm not upset with you Granny for not giving me a good answer, or for thinking you might sometimes snoop if you thought a child was in some kind of danger. You can't help reacting like a grandmother, and most of the times it's good and I like it. And most of all, I want you to know that no matter what you do, I'll always love you.

Love,
Jordy

WHY didn't the skeleton do her homework?
Answer: Because she was a lazy bone.

JORDY

April 27

Dear Granny,

Why are Sarah, Jake and even Darlene ALL jealous of me? I can't believe it, but it's true. It really is!!! They are all jealous of me. And I know it's true because they told me. Can you believe it??? Jealous of ME! But I didn't tell you why — it's because I'm the ONLY — the ONLY — one who gets letters. (I'm not talking about birthday cards or get-well cards.) Can you believe DARLENE does not get even one letter? Jake said he's going to e-mail his grandmother in London and ask her to send him a letter. Sarah didn't say anything, but I know what she was thinking and I bet she's going to do the same thing. Or maybe she'll ask her favorite aunt to write to her, the one who always sends her presents. Anyways I'm very happy! I shouldn't say it — and I WOULDN'T EVER say it to anyone, but it's a good, good feeling when someone is jealous of you. A much, much better feeling than if you are jealous of them. I'm glad I have you, Granny. And I would love you even if you didn't write letters. But don't stop.

When I hear anything exciting, I want to tell you. And if something funny happens, I want to tell you because I know it would make you laugh, too.

Love,
Jordy

P.S. I hope you don't mind, Granny, but sometimes I take some of your letters to school. I just like to talk about them at recess sometimes. And Jake and Sarah like to find WHY jokes for you too, so it's fun.

April 30

Dear Granny,

Michael has this stupid friend, Hank. He's here every Tuesday and Friday, waiting for Michael to come home from baseball practice. I don't like him. He's weird. He always pokes me or tickles me until it hurts. I told Mom I don't like him, but she said we have to be nice to him because his father ran away when he was born and his mother works all day.

I don't care what she said. I don't like him and next time he comes I'll tell him I have to do my homework and go straight to my room.

Nothing much new. Jake, Sarah and I are going to be in the school play which should be a lot of fun.

Love you a lot,
Jordy

Question: Why did the waiter win at tennis?
Answer: Because he had the best serve.

"Michael has this stupid friend, Hank...He always pokes me or tickles me until it hurts."

May 2

Dear Jordy,

You were right when you decided not to be around someone who pokes you and thinks it's funny to tickle you until it hurts. Avoiding Hank by going to your room is an excellent idea. You have good common sense and are right to listen to your feelings.

I am glad you are taking part in the school play. What play will they be performing and what role will you be playing? Your Mom told me that you and Jake are taking karate lessons. How are the lessons going?

I love you and always appreciate and anticipate with such pleasure your letters. (Bad grammar, but the sentiment is sincere and it's not important enough to re-write.)

Love you,
Granny

"You were right when you decided not to be around someone who pokes you and thinks it's funny to tickle you until it hurts."

May 6

Dear Granny,

I was wrong about Hank. He is a really nice guy. I told him I don't like to be poked and it hurts me when he tickles me. He said he was sorry and showed me how he could tickle me so that I can laugh but not so much that it hurts. He was very sorry that he hurt me and offered to take me out for ice cream. He even told me that I can come to his house sometimes to watch videos. He's really cool. Even though he's older than me, he treats me like an equal, not like Michael who always treats me like a kid. I was wrong about him — he's really nice. I think Mom was right; he's lonely and needs friends.

The school play is "Fiddler on the Roof" and they didn't assign the parts yet. Jake says he hopes he doesn't have to dance because he has two left feet.

Love,
Jordy

Question: Why was the post office fat?
Answer: Because it ate too much junk mail.

May 9

Granny,

How could you?! You don't know what you did to me! You told Mom what I wrote you and she went absolutely crazy, asking me questions, telling Michael he can't see Hank again, and giving me lectures about good touch, bad touch — as if I was a baby. Hank didn't do anything and now he can't come to the house again. Michael is mad at me. Diane keeps asking me questions and Mommy acts hysterical when I try to explain that Hank is really a good guy and didn't do anything bad. Dad is mixing in too and lectured to me about "You can't be too careful...blah, blah, blah."

It's totally YOUR fault. You blabbed to Mom when you should have talked to me — not Mom. I thought I could trust you but now I can't. I'm not writing you ever again and I don't want you to write to me.

Jordy

May 12

Dear Jordy,

I apologize. I had no idea the trouble I would cause by telling your mother. I did it because I felt Hank's behavior was totally unacceptable and could lead to unpleasant consequences. I was very concerned and felt your mother needed to know. I thought you and she would sit down quietly and talk about it. Had I known how she would react, I would have flown in to discuss this with you myself – that's how concerned I was. Telephoning you was not a good option because of my hearing difficulties. Letter writing has its limitation and some subjects need to be discussed in person.

Again, I am truly very, very sorry. Please forgive me.

Love,
Granny

"I apologize. I had no idea the trouble I would cause by telling your mother."

May 16

Dear Jordy,

You won't answer my telephone calls. You won't write me. What can I do to convince you that I am truly sorry and want to make it up to you?
If I give up chocolates for a week, would that be enough?
If I give up ice-cream for a month, would that be enough?
And if I give up doing crossword puzzles before going to bed – and you know I can't go to sleep without doing my crossword puzzle – if I give it up for one week, would that be atonement enough?

Please accept my peace offerings and please forgive me.

Love,
Your (truly repentant) Granny

May 19

Jordan,

It's not fair. I apologized. I said I was sorry. I was willing to make amends. And still no word from you.

Everyone makes mistakes. You, me, everyone. The question is, did they mean any harm? I meant no harm, but I made a mistake. Yes, you were right – I should have spoken to you directly, not told your mother – but I didn't, and it's done.

Does that mean I'm not allowed to ever make a mistake?
Does that mean I will never be forgiven?

I miss your letters so much. I miss feeling close to you. I even miss those funny Why jokes. I wish you would forgive me and we could be close again.

Love,
Your truly, truly sorry Granny

May 28

Dear Granny,

I forgive you. I was wrong too. I apologize. Diane said I acted stupid. I didn't tell her, but I think she was right. Like she said, I over-reacted. I'm sorry. Mom fixed things up. She spoke with Hank's mother and it's all over and done with.

Granny, it was really awful without you. I missed you. There was so much I <u>needed</u> to tell you, but I couldn't. Let's be friends again.

I love you sooooo much.

Your good friend and loving grandchild,
Jordy

P.S. Here's a good Why joke:
Why did the vampire get into trouble in Art class?
Because he drew blood.
(A little gory, but funny in a way)

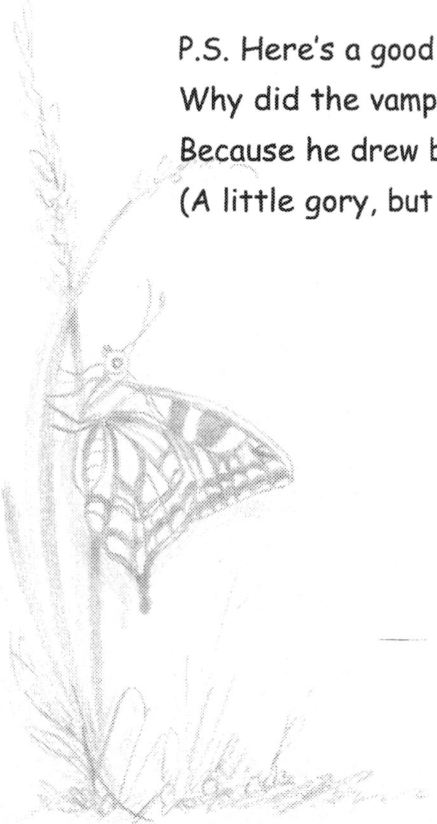

“Granny…I missed you.
Let's be friends again.
I love you sooooo much.”

Dear Jordy, May 31

I am so very, very happy. I too missed you dreadfully. I too want to be friends again.

Your overjoyed and ecstatically happy
Granny

JORDY

June 4

Dear Granny,

I don't know what to do. Whatever I do is wrong. Please tell me what I should do.

Sarah is my best friend after Jake. I caught her vomiting in the bathroom when I went to her house last month. She told me it was because she ate something that wasn't good. I forgot all about it. Then she came to my house and had some chocolate chip cookies and went into the bathroom. I went in after she was finished and it smelled like vomit. I thought maybe she ate too many cookies. And then on Monday we had some cake and milk while we were doing homework, and I caught her vomiting again.

I asked her what was going on and she told me. After she eats, she puts her finger down her throat and makes herself vomit. She says she does it because she's fat and she wants to lose weight. Granny, she's NOT fat. She's thin — she's thinner than Diane and I think she's getting thinner. I tried to tell her but she wouldn't listen. Then she made me PROMISE, CROSS MY HEART AND HOPE TO DIE, AND SWEAR THAT I WOULD NEVER TELL ANYONE.

Granny, I heard Diane talking on the phone and she was telling Marcy about a girl who almost died from Buleemia. This girl ate, vomited, and ate and vomited, and landed up in the hospital and almost died. Granny, could this happen to Sarah?

I know I should tell Mom but I can't — I SWORE. If I tell, Sarah will never trust me again and she won't be my friend any more. And we've been friends since nursery school.

But what if she gets sick and dies? I asked Diane to tell me about Buleemia and what she said sounded just like Sarah. I'm scared. Please answer right away.

Love,
Jordy

P.S. Do you think you could answer me just as soon as you get this letter? Don't phone me because I might have to yell to make you hear, and somebody in the house might hear me.

June 6

Dear Jordy,

You are right to be frightened. You have a very serious choice to make.

But before you decide whether to keep your promise to Sarah, have you tried to persuade her to tell her mother – or some adult she trusts – about her vomiting? Maybe you've tried this and she doesn't want to tell anyone else. This often happens, so you'll still have to make a big decision.

If you tell your mother, Sarah will be mad at you and won't want to be friends any more. You will also feel bad because you swore you would keep her secret and you broke your promise.

But if you don't tell, Sarah could get very sick and need to be hospitalized.

I'm thinking... If you saw your friend crossing the road and a car was coming towards her, would you push her out of the way even though she could fall and hurt herself and blame you?

But perhaps that's not a good example. The choice is simple: You can save your friend at the cost of losing her friendship, or you could say nothing and let her get seriously ill.

I strongly believe the life, the health, of your friend takes precedence (is much more important) than a promise.

Could you ever forgive yourself if Sarah got so sick that they had to take her to the hospital? Would Sarah's parents forgive you?

I have confidence you will make the right decision. But make it very, very soon. The longer Sarah continues to make herself vomit after eating, the harder it will be to cure her.

Let me know very soon about your decision.

Love,
Granny

P.S. I can't understand Sarah's parents not noticing her sudden weight loss. I know her father lost his job, but that can't be the reason for her parents being oblivious to what's going on with their daughter. Possibly it's because they've been so preoccupied with the new baby's colic problem; or possibly because Sarah was able to disguise her weight loss by wearing over-size clothing.

Love,
Granny

Dear Granny, June 9

Why am I writing you this note?
To tell you that Sarah's parents found out about her buleemia. I am so glad I didn't have to tell them. They aren't mad at Sarah, they just want to help. They talked with her about it and they all agreed that the best thing for Sarah to do is to go to a Rehab. So Sarah's going, and she feels good that she's going to get help. Gotta go, lots of homework to do.

Love,
Jordy

JORDY

June 12

Dear Granny,

Why didn't I finish talking to you on the phone? I told you on the phone, but I had to start your letter with a WHY, which is why I did.

Michael started teasing me when he saw me crying while I was talking to you so I had to bang down the phone. He always starts up with me and then Mom blames me when I punch him. But I want to tell you what I was trying to tell you on the phone.

My friend Amy's aunt died and then her uncle went to the hospital and *he* died. Amy said that death comes in threes — and she was afraid who would die next. Then her aunt in Australia died. I didn't believe it, but Jake said it's true — death *always* comes in threes. His hamster died and his father got him another one. The second hamster died soon after that. Jake said to himself, "I wonder who will be next?" It was the canary. He dropped dead. Jake said he *knew* it would happen. He said it's the Rule of Threes again. Remember when I told you he believed in that rule?

And you remember when Uncle Nathan died last year, and now Mom's cousin Beth is very sick and they expect her to die soon. I don't know who will be next.

I told Mom about the Rule of Threes and how I worried about you being next, but she told me not to be stupid, there is no Rule of Threes, stop thinking about nonsense, and that you are not going to die.

How does she know you are not going to die? And it was the way she said it — in an angry voice — the voice she uses when she's worried.

I try not to think about it, but at night I can't help it.

I hope I am not scaring you. Mom says there's no Rule of Threes and I know she is right. So please don't worry because I am sure you will live to be a ripe old age.

I love you very, very, very much and wish you could come to visit.

Jordy

P.S. Do you believe in praying?

June 16

Dear Jordy,

Why does a person ask a question?
Answer: Because they want an answer.

Do I believe in prayer? Yes, I do believe in prayer. I also believe that God gave people a heart and a mind – a heart to feel and a mind to think. It's normal to feel frightened, but when you stop being so frightened, it's time to use your mind. One way is to ask if what you are scared of is true. And it's always better to talk about it with somebody you trust who will take the time to listen to you.

You asked your mother, and that was the right thing to do. But most people, and that includes your mother, are frightened to talk about death – it scares them. They don't like talking or thinking about it. That's why your mother didn't want to hear or talk about my dying. It's scary to think about.

Nobody wants to die unless they are very, very sick and in lots of pain – and even then many people still want to live.

But dying is natural. Everybody dies. Wouldn't it be terrible if everyone lived forever? How could the world hold so many people? How could there be enough food? Most of the people would be so old that they would need younger people to take care of them. There wouldn't be enough young people to do that. Can you imagine such a world? I think it would be absolutely terrible.

Another way of looking at it is that when people die, they make room for babies who are being born. I don't particularly like that answer, but it's an answer.

Many people believe that when you die, your soul lives on. I believe that. I truly believe that even though the body dies, the soul always lives on.

Some people believe in reincarnation – that means they believe that after a person dies, his or her soul goes into the unborn body which then comes back to earth in another form. Doesn't that sound interesting – being born again in another body? Imagine, one could be an astronaut in one lifetime, a president of a country in another, or one could be born anywhere on earth – Africa, Asia or North American. One could be born as a woman or a man, be white, Chinese, or black – wow!

> "Do I believe in prayer? Yes, I do believe in prayer. I also believe that God gave people a heart and a mind - a heart to feel and a mind to think."

Coming back as another person in another lifetime sounds exciting. But even though a lot of people believe in reincarnation, I'm not sure I believe in it.

What I do believe is that God gave us the precious gift of life to enjoy and to learn, and if you follow the Ten Commandments you can live a good life and help other people, too.

I intend to live a long, long time so it's not something I need to be worried about.

But when the time comes to die – a time that comes to every single person – I will be sad because I don't want to leave all the people I so dearly love. I know you will be sad when I die, and that hurts me. But afterwards, when time passes, I hope you will have happy thoughts about me – happy memories of the time we spent together, the fun we had with our WHY letters. Even if you still have sad thoughts sometimes, you might be happy for me that I didn't live forever, to get older and older, sicker and sicker, more and more frail and helpless.

When I was in school I took a course called Philosophy 101. The professor said that death was important because it makes life more valuable. He said that knowing that life will not go on forever makes one appreciate the precious gift of life. I didn't fully understand that when he said it, but as I get older I realize more and more that life is precious and that one has to be so *grateful for the blessing of life – and for me, one of the most wonderful gifts life has given me is having you as my grandchild. I love you so very, very much.*

I hope what I have written makes sense to you. Let's talk more about it when we visit during your summer vacation.

Love,
Granny

P.S. I don't believe the Rule of Threes exists. But why don't YOU check it out to be absolutely certain it's not true. Why don't you go on the Internet and Google it to find out for yourself?

> "What I do believe is that God gave us the precious gift of life to enjoy and to learn..."

JORDY

June 19

Dear Granny,

Why do I feel better now?
Because your letter made me feel better.

Maybe I'll have some more questions when we go on vacation.
I don't know.

For now I can't wait to go with you to London next month and see all the sights. Jake says London is an AWESOME city. He was there with his family last year and he almost saw the queen, but she didn't come out of her castle that day. Maybe I'll have a chance to see her.

I'm counting the days...

Love,
Jordy

P.S. I just thought of a question. I know it's stupid, but I'll ask anyhow. When Uncle Joe died and went to heaven, do you think he saw Aunt Jenny there?

June 23

Dear Jordy,

Of course Uncle Joe saw Aunt Jenny there. Would Aunt Jenny ever not greet anyone who came to the door?

Love you, and I too am counting the days. Do you want me to send you any brochures about London?

Love,
Granny

P.S. Jordy, I was in a restaurant that had a menu for children and saw placemats with riddles on them. I looked at a placemat and had such a pleasant surprise because there was a WHY question on it. I immediately thought of you and wrote it down so I would remember. Here is what it asked:

Why are worms always depressed?
Answer: Because they don't have a funny bone in their body.

June 27

Dear Jordy,

Why am I so happy? Because I am looking forward with much anticipation to our visiting London together in a few more weeks.

There are so many wonderful sights to see. Our first stop will be Buckingham Palace where the Queen lives. We can see the changing of the guards. It's so exciting to see them galloping in unison on their horses. If we are lucky, we can see them in their special uniforms – metal helmets with bright red feathers bobbing up and down or the foot soldiers wearing those big furry hats called busbies. They are so big they can hardly see as they march in formation and stamp their feet as they choose two special officers, called sentries, to be on duty to guard the palace. We can even go into the palace and see the beautiful pictures and furniture and maybe meet the Queen – but you really have to be lucky to meet her.

Our next stop will be the Tower of London where in olden times they kept their prisoners. It's got a big turret and a very special bridge and the guards there look really old-fashioned in their straw hats, tunics, and britches.

Be sure to bring a camera because you just can't describe to your friends how different they look from anything you've seen. They even carry special swords, but of course don't use them.

Next I think we will stop at Madame Tussauds Museum where every celebrity from film stars to famous football players are on display. Of course Princess Diana and the Queen are there. They look so real you can almost believe that you are standing in front of the real person.

They have a fabulously fun Victorian ride through the streets of London at night which is really magical. Next stop – we haven't had lunch yet so we will go to Harrods, a beautiful department store where they have 20 restaurants with all sorts of goodies. We could have hot chocolate there with sandwiches and scones and see all the magnificent sweets, chocolates and cakes on display. It will make your mouth water just to look at them...yum, yum.

We haven't talked about museums. You'll love the Science Museum because it has a space ship and a lot of interactive activities. The Victoria and Albert Museum is full of wonderful treasures to buy in their gift shop and has such beautiful costumes and dresses of all the princesses and the Queen.

Perhaps we will go to a fun fair with lots of rides or see another castle called Windsor Castle, the summer house of the Queen. They have the most fabulous doll house there, with everything miniature from chandeliers and golden coaches to golden cutlery, pots, pans and pictures.

But I've got to leave a few things as a surprise so I won't give you any more clues as to what we will do except I promise you'll really enjoy your trip to London.

Can't wait to get started on this adventure! See you very soon.

Lots of love,
Granny

I love you Granny!
xoxoxoxoxo
Jordy
J
...the end.

Acknowledgments

I would like to thank Adam, my husband, my friend, my mentor, and, as always, "The wind beneath my wings."

To Kathryn Donatelli, artistc extraordinaire, for her absolutely exquisite illustrations and for bringing the characters to life.

I am indebted to my marvelous editor, Martha Jablow, for her expertise and most helpful suggestions, which made the task of writing so much easier.

To Sandra Zierdt, outstanding graphic artist, many thanks for the excellent book design.

To my computer wizard, Karen Strauss, thank you for always being there in an emergency.

To encourage closer communication between grandparents and grandchildren, several pages are left blank for the readers to jot notes or draft letters of their own